Jordan

by Corey Anderson

Consultant: Marjorie Faulstich Orellana, PhD
Professor of Urban Schooling
University of California, Los Angeles

BEARPORT PUBLISHING

New York, New York

Credits

Cover, © mustafagull/iStock and © tenkl/Shutterstock; TOC, © netzach farbiash/Wikimedia; 4, © benedek/ Getty Images; 5T, © Juliane Thiere/Alamy; 5B, © Richard Yoshida/Shutterstock; 7, © renan gicquel/Getty Images; 8T, © yeowatzup/Wikimedia; 8B, © omardajani/Shutterstock; 9, © Alexey Stiop/Dreamstime; 10, © Vickey Chauhan/Shutterstock; 11T, © Alexandr Junek Imaging/Shutterstock; 11B, © Nimit Virdi/Getty Images; 12, © RnDmS/Getty Images; 13, © Crazy nook/Shutterstock; 14T, © toni salvatella/Getty Images; 14B, © World History Archive/Newscom/Newscom; 15, © Oleh_Slobodeniuk/Getty Images; 16–17, © tenki/Shutterstock; 18T, © Melih Cevdet Teksen/Shutterstock; 18B, © ZouZou/Shutterstock; 19, © Ehab Othman/Shutterstock; 20T, © Wakllaff/Shutterstock; 20B, © Olga Savina/Shutterstock; 21, © Zurijeta/Shutterstock; 22, © Manuel ROMARIS/Getty Images; 23, © Richard Yoshida/Shutterstock; 24, © Anton_Ivanov/Shutterstock; 25T, © GranTotufo/ Shutterstock; 25B, © bumihills/Shutterstock; 26, © bonchan/Getty Images; 27T, © Joel Carillet/Getty Images; 27B, © KVLADIMIRV/Getty Images; 28, © Salah Malkawi/Getty Images; 29T, © Christopher Furlong/Getty Images; 29B, © Tamara Didenko/Shutterstock; 30M, © oconnelll/Shutterstock; 30B, © Ken Walker/Wikimedia; 31 (T to B), © World History Archive/Newscom, © Manuel ROMARIS/Getty Images, © Ehab Othman/Shutterstock, © Vickey Chauhan/Wikimedia, and © Stefan Cristian Cioata/Getty Images; 32, © spatuletail/Shutterstock.

Publisher: Kenn Goin
Senior Editor: Joyce Tavolacci
Creative Director: Spencer Brinker
Design: Debrah Kaiser
Photo Researcher: Book Buddy Media

Library of Congress Cataloging-in-Publication Data

Names: Anderson, Corey, author.
Title: Jordan / by Corey Anderson.
Description: New York, New York : Bearpoint Publishing Company, [2020] | Series: Countries we come from | Includes bibliographical references and index.
Identifiers: LCCN 2019014373 (print) | LCCN 2019018594 (ebook) | ISBN 9781642805857 (ebook) | ISBN 9781642805314 (library)
Subjects: LCSH: Jordan—Juvenile literature.
Classification: LCC DS153 (ebook) | LCC DS153 .A73 2020 (print) | DDC 956.95—dc23
LC record available at https://lccn.loc.gov/2019014373

For more information, write to Bearport Publishing Company, Inc., 45 West 21st Street, Suite 3B, New York, New York 10010. Printed in the United States of America.

10 9 8 7 6 5 4 3 2 1

Contents

This Is Jordan

SUNNY

Joyful

ANCIENT

Jordan is a country in the Middle East.
Over 10 million people live there.

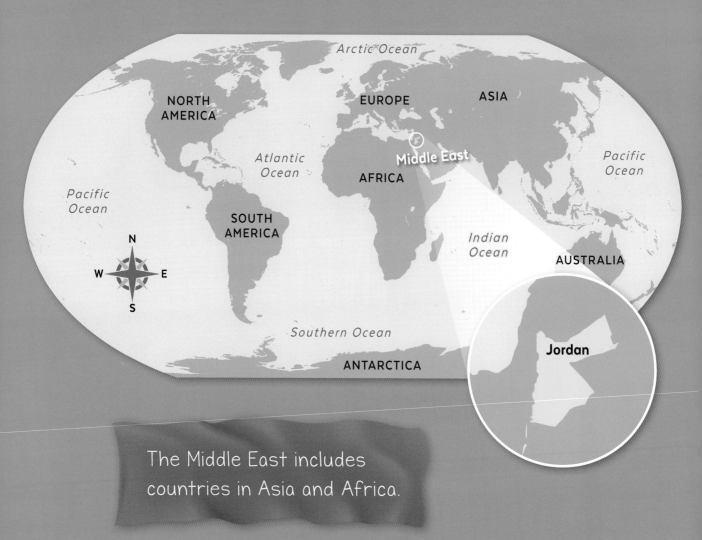

The Middle East includes
countries in Asia and Africa.

the city of
Amman in Jordan

A huge desert covers much of Jordan.

Syrian Desert

Most cities and farmland lie in the west, in the Jordan Valley.

The Jordan River flows through the Jordan Valley. The river provides fresh water to many Jordanians.

Interesting animals live in Jordan.
Striped hyenas **scavenge** for food.

Sand cats hunt for small animals.

Ostriches dart across the land.

Persian sand cat

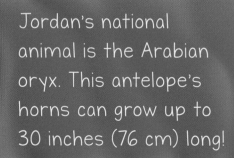

Jordan's national animal is the Arabian oryx. This antelope's horns can grow up to 30 inches (76 cm) long!

The Dead Sea is in western Jordan.
It's a huge, salty lake.

The Dead Sea is so salty that fish and plants cannot live in it.

People enjoy swimming in the lake.

The water's high salt content makes it easy to float!

Humans have lived in Jordan for tens of thousands of years.

These early people left **artifacts** behind, such as tools.

an ancient tool used to grind flour

In 2018, scientists found 14,000-year-old fireplaces with bread inside!

Jordanians were some of the first people to keep cats as pets.

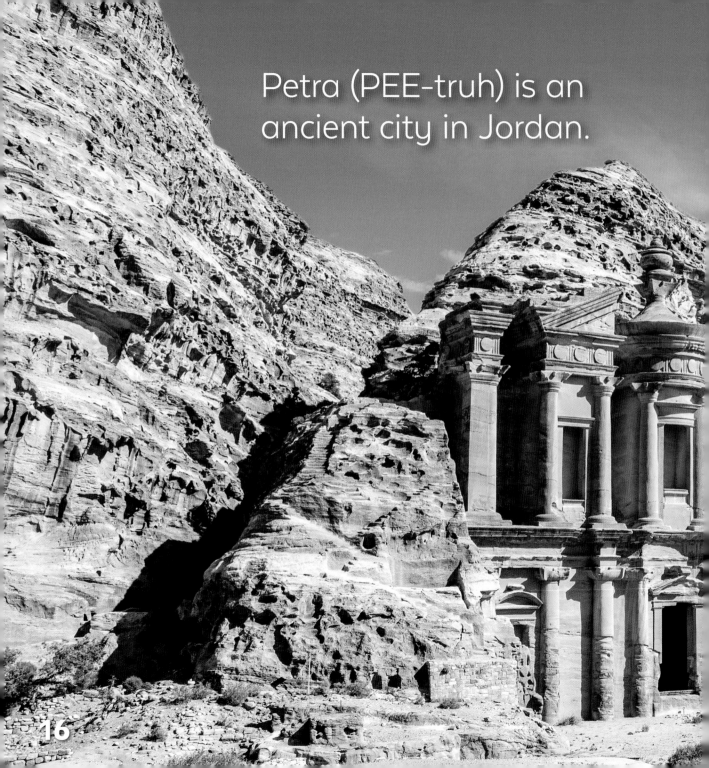

Petra (PEE-truh) is an ancient city in Jordan.

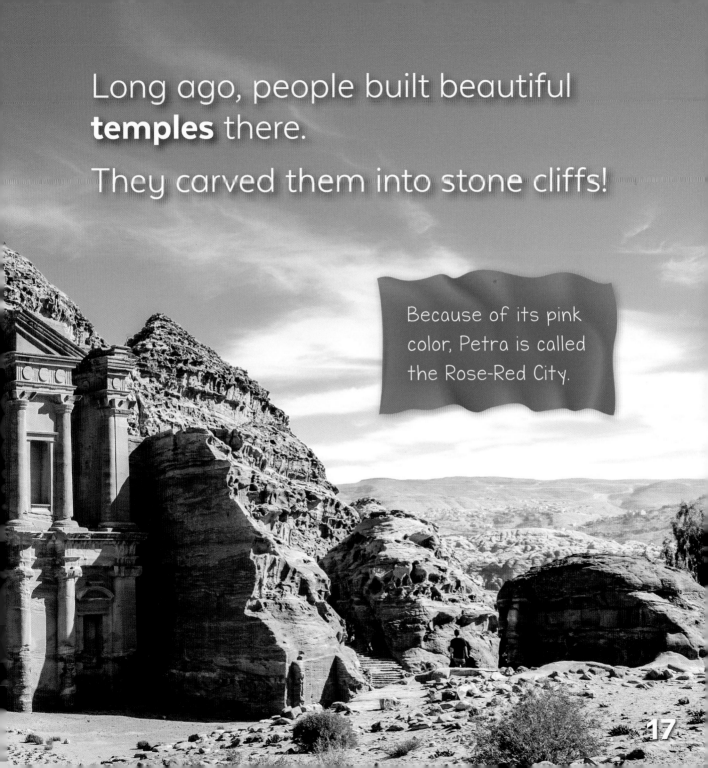

Long ago, people built beautiful **temples** there.

They carved them into stone cliffs!

Because of its pink color, Petra is called the Rose-Red City.

Today, the people of Jordan include **refugees**.

Many are from Palestine or Syria.

Most of the people who live in Jordan follow the religion of Islam.

Refugees often leave their home countries because of war or hunger.

refugees from Syria

19

Jordan's main language is Arabic.

This is how you say *cat* in Arabic:

Qut (CUT)

This is how you say *dog*:

Alkalb
(al-KAL-bul)

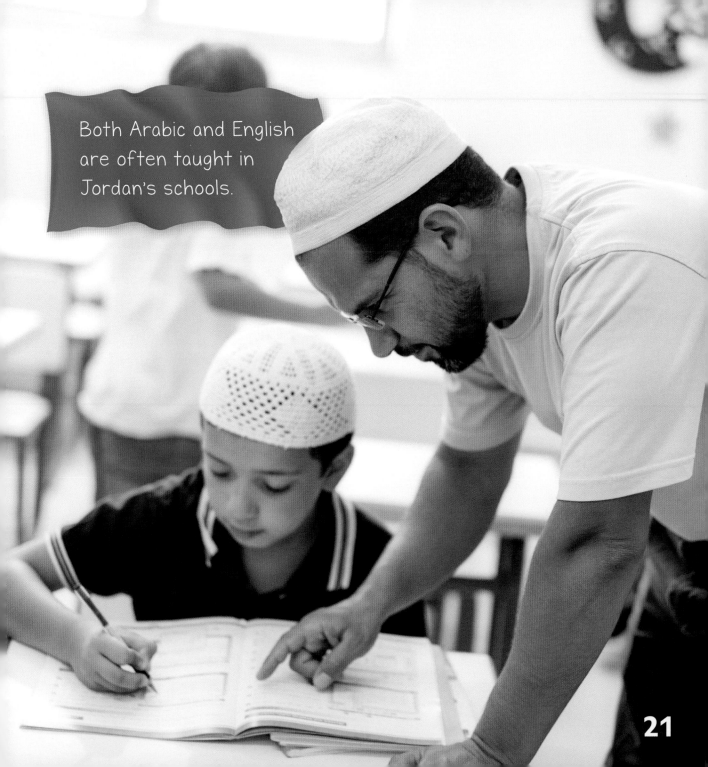

Both Arabic and English are often taught in Jordan's schools.

21

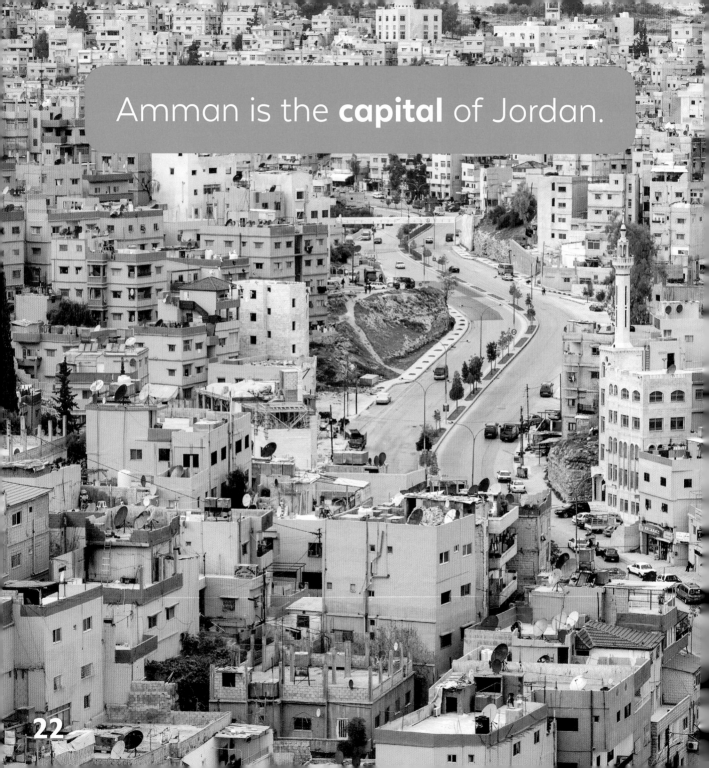

Amman is the **capital** of Jordan.

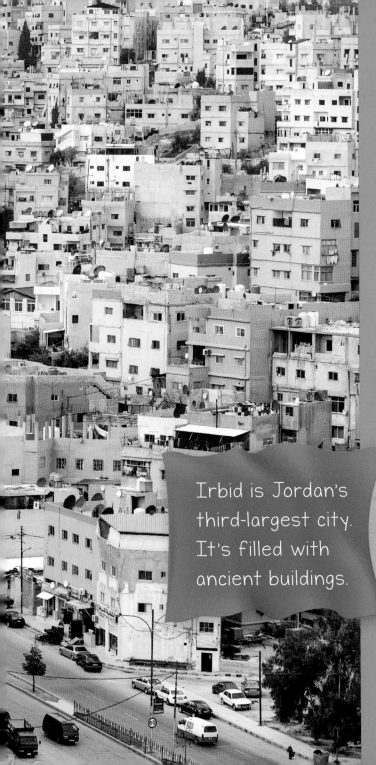

Over four million people live there.

That's close to half of all the people in Jordan!

Irbid is Jordan's third-largest city. It's filled with ancient buildings.

What clothing do Jordanians wear?

Men usually wear a long headdress called a kaffiyeh (cuh-FEE-yuh).

A kaffiyeh protects a person's face from the sun and blowing sand.

kaffiyeh

Women often wear dresses and headscarves.

In central Jordan, women sometimes wear dresses with very long sleeves. The sleeves can be up to 10 feet (3 m) long!

Food in Jordan is rich and tasty.

Mansaf (MAHN-sahf) is lamb cooked in yogurt sauce.

It's served on a big tray of rice.

Muhallabia (moo-heh-LEH-bee-uh) is a sweet, creamy pudding.

Many Jordanians enjoy eating hummus. It's a thick spread made from chickpeas.

It's time to race!

Many Jordanians love camel and horse racing.

Camels can run around 40 miles per hour (64 kph).

Sometimes, small robots race the animals!

robot

Jordanians treasure Arabian horses. These beautiful animals can run up to 50 miles per hour (81 kph).

Fast Facts

Capital city: Amman

Population of Jordan: Over 10 million

Main language: Arabic

Money: Jordanian dinar

Major religion: Islam

Neighboring countries: Iraq, Israel, Saudi Arabia, and Syria

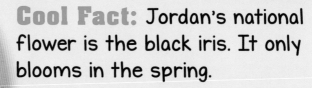

Cool Fact: Jordan's national flower is the black iris. It only blooms in the spring.

artifacts (ART-ih-facts) objects that were made by people in the past

capital (KAP-uh-tuhl) the city where a country's government is based

refugees (ref-yuh-JEEZ) people who are forced to leave their country

scavenge (SKAV-enj) to search for and feed on dead animals

temples (TEMP-ulz) buildings used as places of worship

31

Index

Read More

Pundyk, Grace. *Welcome to Jordan (Welcome to My Country).* Milwaukee, WI: Gareth Stevens (2004).

Rechner, Amy. *Jordan (Country Profiles).* Minneapolis, MN: Bellwether (2018).

Learn More Online

To learn more about Jordan, visit
www.bearportpublishing.com/CountriesWeComeFrom

About the Author

Corey Anderson is a writer from Los Angeles who loves exploring destinations near and far with her husband, Josh, and sons, Leo and Dane.